Actual Jokes, M[...] and Other Minutiae

Tony Batory

The opinions expressed in this manuscript are solely the opinions of the author and do not represent the opinions or thoughts of the publisher. The author has represented and warranted full ownership and/or legal right to publish all the materials in this book.

Actuarial Jokes, Memoirs and Other Minutiae
All Rights Reserved.
Copyright © 2015 Tony Batory
v4.0

Cover Illustration © 2015 Tod G. Smith. All rights reserved - used with permission.

This book may not be reproduced, transmitted, or stored in whole or in part by any means, including graphic, electronic, or mechanical without the express written consent of the publisher except in the case of brief quotations embodied in critical articles and reviews.

Outskirts Press, Inc.
http://www.outskirtspress.com

ISBN: 978-1-4787-5512-8

Outskirts Press and the "OP" logo are trademarks belonging to Outskirts Press, Inc.

PRINTED IN THE UNITED STATES OF AMERICA

I would like to thank my wife Nancy and my sons Tyler and Brandon. Although they are not actuaries in any sense of the word, they provided the actuarial inspiration for much of this book.

Thanks to Olga Jacobs who constantly encouraged me to keep writing,

And thanks to Tod Smith for the cover illustration.

Table of Contents

1. Reflections at Crunch Time 1
2. To Rate Or Not To Rate 5
3. Puzzles and Word Searches 7
4. Jokes, Jokes, Jokes –
   Dilbert Could Have Been an Actuary 12
5. 2 + 2 17
6. Actuarial Communications 20
7. Is Technology Overrated? 23
8. U Cant Rate This, Actuarial Rap – Music 1 26
9. Y2K = YUK. Joea – A Scifi Short Story 28
10. Actuarialogos 37
11. The Sunny Actuary – Music 2 51
12. You Can't Be Serious 53
13. National Health Care Debate 1 –
    the Reformist vs. the Actuary 56
14. National Health Care Debate 2 –
    the Consultant vs. the In House Actuary 60

15. National Health Care Debate 3 –
    the Doctor vs. the Actuary..................................70
16. National Health Care Debate 4 –
    the Politician vs. the Actuary..............................74
17. Bell Curve 78
18. Imprudent Immeasurables 81
19. Ode to an Actuarial Student..84
20. Tales from Inside the Box (Elevator)...............................87
21. A Trip to the Grocery Store..91
22. Actuarial Insults..94
23. Advanced Calculus..98
24. Actuarial Bucket List 101

CHAPTER 1
REFLECTIONS AT CRUNCH TIME

THERE ARE MANY types of actuaries, casualty or life, consulting or insurance, big A or little a. But I'm like to propose a new type of categorization based on preference in communication tool. Personally, I'm a WP actuary. I use a wood pencil.

Before I relate the events that drove home the significance of this 'point', first let me say that it has been my observation that most actuaries use pen. In the midst of advances in computers and changing actuarial roles, some actuaries consciously or unconsciously pursue an aura of infallibility drawn in ink. The real question is whether this goal has become passé in today's business environment. With mergers and acquisitions happening all around us, even actuaries get downsized and with that vulnerability, fallibility logically follows. The rising fortunes of accountants and doctors have reduced the awe of the actuary. Besides, how can we learn from our mistakes if we never make any?

Many of my colleagues opt for mechanical pencils. That's a cop out. Some of these MP's don't even have erasers-which defeats the whole purpose of pencil. The apparent advantage of not having to sharpen the thing is illusory, since the uniformly thin lead frequently breaks leaving minute chunks of lead scattered across the horizon of your workstation. And more importantly, these constant interruptions to your workflow are counterproductive. Don't underestimate the conduit of your creativity. An engineer at Lehigh University once told me that no mechanical pencil could ever replicate the feel of a 'real' pencil in your hand. It's true; nothing can replace the feeling of a new, freshly sharpened WP. The subtle aroma of freshly cut wood mixed with a touch of lead even has psychological benefits. Like Pavlov's dogs, one whiff and my logical processes start salivating.

But the recent business environment yielded even more applications. Though I have never been laid off or changed jobs, I have worked for four different companies in four years. With the owner du jour expressing a special interest in my current project, our weekly status meeting grew tense when a critical miscommunication made missing our deadline a possibility. Contributing to the anxiety was a 20oz. cafeteria coffee that has been known to dissolve plastic spoons and an adrenalin build-up from having to sit quietly while our contract lawyer tediously outlined the problem.

Cigarettes are out of the question and gum is rude. With no other outlet, I found myself chewing through my pencil. First the eraser, then the metal band and finally the wood itself. A symbolic taste of ashes became a real taste of lead as I fretted about our blown project. But the tension release was valuable. And consider the potential damage that an MP would have made to my $800 dental crown. Consider the embarrassment had the lead dust that settled in my beard, been ink. In fact it merely added a steely sort of distinguished look, reminiscent of the gray hairs that this project was adding to the heads and faces of my colleagues. That inspired discussion about a new of insurance-related hair coloring products which would come in the traditional colors of white or grey, as well as a new tint for the aspiring analyst, lead. The marketing slogan would be 'Only your actuary knows for sure'.

When I returned to my desk and stared at the jagged end of my pencil, the consequences of 'crunch time' became physically apparent. Something possessed me to shove that jagged end into my electric sharpener (which has prominent positioning at my workstation). Out came a double edged sword, a fitting symbol of the project that we were working on, and of actuarial prowess in general: how to turn adversity into flexibility.

Now when someone asks me a question, I can look at the problem from a different perspective; perhaps the answer is both yes and no. Reworking a set of rates? No problem, I just invert my pencil. Does this really produce different answers? Our actuarial research area could test if one side of the pencil were more conservative than the other.

My new device also served as a reminder of the people that were pulling overtime on this project. While they were burning the candle at both ends, I was sharpening my pencil at both ends.

Well, our project turned out okay, we made our deadline. And while there was a lot of hard work from a lot of people, I don't discount the role of my two-sided WP. So now I am a confirmed WP purist although not always two-sided. And while a matched set of MP's might make a nice wedding present when two actuaries get married, it stretches the point considerably, dangerous for a pencil. (Side note: how do these actuarial couples decide who does their taxes?).

In short, the permanence of ink is unsuitable in a flexible business environment. And though computer technology will doubtless continue to advance, there will always be a place for the WP-in my heart, in my hand and between my teeth.

Originally published in May/June 1996 issue of Contingencies

CHAPTER 2
TO RATE OR NOT TO RATE

To rate or not to rate, that is the question. Whether 'tis nobler in mind to suffer the slings and arrows of outrageous change requests or to deploy untested code. What's to come is still unsure; in delay there lies no plenty. It is a tale told by an underwriter, full of sound and fury, signifying nothing. Friends, programmers, actuaries, lend me your passwords. I come to bury the old process, not to praise it. For all the systems are a stage and the tables its' actors. So, once more unto the testing, the version's afoot. A rel, a rel, my kingdom for a rel. Yes actuaries, there are more things in heaven and earth than dreamt of by your rate cards. If you email us, do we not reply; if you text us, do we not text back? Age cannot wither our system, nor documentation stale her infinite variety. Now is the winter of our discontent made glorious by this sun of technology. Arise fair sun and kill the envious moon and delete all that redundant data.

Alas, poor Tony, I knew him well.

CHAPTER 3
Puzzles and Word Searches

TONY, OLGA, DIANE, Linda and Meredith are health actuaries, pricing five different products for five different locations, for five different effective dates. From the information provided, determine who is pricing what (Health Spending Account, indemnity, PPO, point of service and HMO) for where (Arizona, California, New York, Texas and Nationwide) and for when (Jan, Feb, Apr, May and Jun).

1. Olga (who isn't pricing HMO) is targeting a January effective date. Linda isn't the person pricing California for May.

2. Meredith's rates are effective exactly two months after the HSA.

3. Arizona's rates will be effective after the HMO rates.

4. Linda is not pricing for February. Meredith isn't pricing

PPO (which is not being priced for NY).

5. Diane's indemnity rates will be effective at least two months before the nationwide product.

You may find the following chart to be helpful, X for no, * for yes.

	NW	AZ	CA	NY	TX	Jan	Feb	Apr	May	Jun	Ind	HSA	POS	PPO	HMO
Tony															
Olga															
Diane															
Meredith															
Linda															
Indemnity															
HSA															
POS															
PPO															
HMO															
Jan															
Feb															
Apr															
May															
Jun															

Any resemblance to real actuaries is just a coincidence.

Puzzles and Word Searches

ACTUARIAL WORD SEARCH - unused letters spell the secret phrase

M	A	O	T	U	A	N	E	T	N	E	M	T	S	E	V	N	I
O	A	S	I	G	N	Y	T	R	E	P	O	R	P	A	F	O	C
R	N	T	R	E	N	D	R	E	B	M	U	N	R	I	S	I	X
B	T	O	H	U	A	O	E	R	O	N	L	Y	V	Y	N	T	L
I	H	T	I	E	N	V	I	R	O	N	M	E	N	T	E	A	I
D	E	A	O	T	M	P	T	T	W	M	O	D	E	L	V	L	A
I	A	L	R	I	A	A	S	A	R	I	N	E	A	E	F	B
T	L	A	A	R	L	S	T	V	G	U	I	E	R	U	S	N	I
Y	T	S	T	I	P	A	N	I	E	N	L	T	R	S	N	I	L
E	H	S	T	H	R	E	E	E	C	R	I	A	E	A	E	I	I
N	S	Y	L	L	A	T	X	U	P	S	A	N	V	C	O	S	T
Y	M	E	D	A	C	A	A	D	E	M	O	G	R	A	P	H	Y
M	I	S	Y	S	T	E	M	S	M	H	O	M	E	A	B	E	E
T	A	B	L	E	I	R	O	Y	T	E	I	C	O	S	E	N	N
D	L	O	S	S	C	I	T	S	I	T	A	T	S	M	E	M	O
E	C	I	N	T	E	G	R	A	T	I	O	N	A	I	D	E	M

WORD LIST

ACADEMY	INFLATION	MONEY	STATISTICS
AUTO	INSURE	MORBIDITY	SYSTEMS
AVERAGE	INTEGRATION	MORTALITY	TABLE
CASUALTY	INTEREST	NINE	TALLY
CLAIMS	INVESTMENT	NUMBER	TAX
COMPENSATION	LIABILITY	ONLY	TEN
COST	LIFE	PARTS	THREE
DEMOGRAPHY	LOSS	PROPERTY	TOIL
EARNINGS	MALPRACTICE	RATE	TOTAL
ENVIRONMENT	MATHEMATICS	SEVEN	TREND
EXAM	MEAN	SIGN	TRIAL
FIVE	MEDIAN	SIX	UNDERWRITE
HEALTH	MEMO	SOCIETY	UNIT
HOME	MODEL	SOLD	VALUATION
			VARY

9

SOLUTION TO THE ACTULOGIC PUZZLE:

May [CA(1)] isn't Linda (1), Olga [Jan(1)], Meredith [no March](2), or Diane [Jun last] (5); it's Tony.

Feb [after only Jan] isn't Meredith (2) or Linda (4); it's Diane [indemnity (5)].

Apr isn't Meredith [HSA would be Feb {indemnity}(2)]; it's Linda.

June is Meredith so HSA is Apr (2).

Jun [last, Meredith] isn't HMO (3) or PPO (4); it's POS.

Jan [Olga] isn't HMO(1); it's PPO. May is HMO, so AZ is Jun [last] (3).

Jan [1st, PPO] isn't NY(4) or NW(5); it's TX.

Feb [Diane] isn't NW(5); it's NY. Apr is NW.

Puzzles and Word Searches

Summary,
Tony, CA, May, HMO
Olga, TX, Jan, PPO
Diane, NY, Feb, indemnity
Meredith, AZ, Jun, POS
Linda, NW, Apr, HSA

Solution to the Word Search – ACTUARIES ARE NUMBER ONE

CHAPTER 4
JOKES, JOKES, JOKES – DILBERT COULD HAVE BEEN AN ACTUARY

HOW MANY NATIONAL account actuaries does it take to change a light bulb? The same number as last year times a trend factor.

How many small group actuaries does it take to change a light bulb? 10, one to screw the light bulb and 9 to interpret the health reform regulations on light bulbs and screwing.

How many management actuaries does it take to change a light bulb? 20, one to screw the light bulb and 19 to have a staff meeting on it.

JOKES, JOKES, JOKES

How many casualty actuaries does it take to change a light bulb? None, the light bulbs are all broken.

How many pension actuaries does it take to change a light bulb? None, they can make an assumption that the light bulb changes itself.

How many healthcare actuaries does it take to change a light bulb?

- None, after credibility weighting, we have indications that the bulb is still lit.
- OR
- None, the department of insurance is not allowing any modifications to the bulb at this time.

Two actuaries are coming out of work. One starts to get into his car but the other gets on a bike. The first actuary says 'what's with the bike, is that something new?' The second actuary says 'Yea, strangest thing happened yesterday. A woman rode up to me on this bike. She must have been one of those 'occupy wall street' protestors. She threw the bike down on the ground, rips off her clothes and throws them on the ground. Then she puts her hands in the air and yells TAKE WHAT YOU WANT. So I took the bike.' The first actuary says 'that was good choice, the clothes probably wouldn't fit.'

This joke also works with accountants, engineers and math teachers.

A philosopher, a lawyer and an healthcare actuary are marooned on a desert isle after a cruise ship wreck and they debate having a wife vs a girlfriend. The philosopher says, 'having a wife is morally and ethically correct and the consistency and long term commitment are good things.' The lawyer says 'I've handled divorces and they're messy, emotional and financially, not worth the risk of marriage. So it's better to have girlfriend.' The healthcare actuary says 'you must have both a wife and a girlfriend.' The others ask him how he came to that conclusion and he says 'you can tell your wife you need to spend more time with your friends. You tell your girlfriend that you need to spend more time with your family. Then you can spend all your time working on healthcare reform.'

An infinite number of actuaries walk into a bar. The first orders a martini, the 2nd a half martini, the 3rd quarter martini, the 4th an eighth martini. The bartender says 'ok, ok, I get it.' And he makes 2 martinis.

An actuary, a physicist and a mathematician walk into a bar. You would think one of them would have ducked.

Actuarialimerick
There once was a nerd from Decator
Who got a state job reviewing insurers.
He wrote regulations
With confused gyrations,
And was nicknamed the IRREGULATOR.

If irreverent priests are defrocked, and dishonest attorneys are disbarred, shouldn't difficult actuaries be deactivated?

Hope you celebrated the St Actuary's day on August 15. It was originally known as the Feast of the Assumption.

Three healthcare actuaries are at heaven's gate and are being questioned by St. Peter on the usefulness of their lives. The first healthcare actuary says, "I deployed ACR rating to comply with federal regs." so St. Peter says, "Fine, welcome to heaven." The second actuary says, "I discovered a new forecasting technique that predicts claims more accurately," so St. Peter says, "Fine, welcome to heaven." The third actuary says, "I invented HMOs." St. Peter says, "Fine, you may stay three days, but then you have to leave."

Rule of Healthcare Reform: If it seems easy, you're doing it wrong.

An actuarial student went into a bookstore and brought two copies of "Actuarial Science for Dummies" at $16.99 each. The total was $50.

Why did the actuary list the nudist colony as bad risk?

The rates were insufficient to cover the exposure.

Side question: what's the SIC for a nudist colony? 7033, for real.

A programmer goes to the store for a loaf of bread. Their spouse says if they have eggs buy a dozen. The programmer comes home with a dozen loaves of bread.

CHAPTER 5
2 + 2

THERE'S AN OLD joke that a CEO wants to know how much is 2+2. They ask various professionals who give different answers. Then an actuary answers 'how much do you want it to be?' THAT'S NOT WHAT HAPPENS IN 2012.

In 2012, the CEO becomes aware of the problem 2 + 2 =? because of legal or publicity issues. The CEO doesn't have a clue, really. So they trickle their intent down to various staff members who file a project request. After a lengthy documentation and funding review, concerns about relevance and cost are overridden by the mandate, 'the CEO wants this answered.' Funding is approved; the project team is assembled and weighs in with various opinions.

The Project Manager says 'it doesn't matter what the answer is, we'll need daily status meetings/updates to track progress.'

The Systems Analysts search the entire internet. And they

say 'the answer is between 3.98 and 4.02.'

The Testing leader says 'I don't know what the answer is, but we'll need at least 100 scenarios to test it thoroughly and comply with Sarbanes-Oxley.'

The Product Analyst says 'we're not sure exactly what you mean by 2+2, so we'll to ask our Legal area for an opinion.'

The lawyers say 'we'll research it and get back to you in 6 months. Don't do anything in the interim.'

The Operations area says 'we need to address existing customers, so we will do a manual workaround and come up with something close. Just don't ask for a definition of 'close' .

The Underwriter says 'the answer will depend on what our competition does and what state regulators tell us. '

Finally after weeks of nervous discussion, they ask the actuary and she immediately responds 'we don't need any system enhancements, the answer is 4'. They mistake her confidence for arrogance and ask 'are you absolutely, positively, 100% certain'? The actuary is a statistician so she knows that nothing is 100% certain. She's also very honest, so she responds, 'no I am not 100% certain'. At that point, the project team completely ignores the actuary.

2 + 2

This story is FYE (for your entertainment) only; any resemblance to existing projects or actuaries is merely coincidental. This story, excluding attachments, does not include confidential and/or proprietary information, and may be used by the any person, entity, or lifeform. If the reader of this story is the intended recipient or his, her or its authorized agent, the reader is hereby, thereby and whereby notified that any dissemination, disintegration, distribution or copying of this story is hunky dory. If you are reading this story in error, please do not notify the author by replying to this message via email, vmail, imail nor smail.

CHAPTER 6
ACTUARIAL COMMUNICATIONS

I RECEIVED A Voice Mail (VM) from Keena in the San Francisco sales office. She was obviously in a big hurry since she didn't leave her last name and she rattled off her phone number so fast I couldn't understand it despite my repeating the message several times. Her message was 'I am getting some funny rates' out of our proposal system. No policy number or anything specific about what was funny. Feeling lucky, I punched in some numbers, and hit on the right number on the second try. But I didn't get Keena, I got her VM. I left a message asking for more detail on the problem and finished with 'Can you please leave your full name and enunciate your phone number more clearly?' I realized after I hung up that I may have been projecting an attitude and the enunciate comment could even be taken as a ethnic slur if you were hypersensitive.

I also included my fax number in the message and sure

enough Keena faxed me back. But since she didn't call, I didn't know the fax was coming. I do make a point of going to my mailbox once a day to throw away my mail. But it has never been a high priority and on this particluar day I was tied up and never got to it. When I picked up the fax the next day, I noticed the key item to look up what was rated, the proposal number, was illegible.

So I called Keena back, but didn't get Keena. I got Kenna's VM; 'Keena will be out of the office for the next couple of days but leave a message anyway.' So I left a message asking for further clarification. And I tried to make a joke to avoid projecting an attitude. This time after I hung up I realized I must have sounded like an idiot.

Keena called me back but didn't get me, she got my VM. Of course local time was 6:56 PM. The next morning when I picked up this message, I tried to email her some documentation. Fortunately, I had the correct spelling from the fax and didn't have to try 'Lee' or 'Li' or 'Lei' or Keena with a Q (there was no Q on the phone at that time). But I still couldn't find her address. Maybe Keena is a nickname and she's in the system under her real name, like 'Tock-sing Li'. Or maybe she's not on the same email system at all. After 15 minutes, I gave up and called Keena directly but didn't get Keena, I got her VM. Of course, local time was 4:36 AM.

In short, there was no problem with the rates just a subtle

misinterpretation of exactly what was being rated. But from the time Keena held up her proposal to the time she got resolution was five business days. This is totally unacceptable by almost any standard. This is not an indictment of Keena or me because from one point of view, it was amazing there was a resolution at all. Keena and I have never spoken to each other.

CHAPTER 7
IS TECHNOLOGY OVERRATED?

INFORMATION TECHNOLOGY HAS come to the front of the healthcare reform debate, and a recent article[1] underlines a recurring theme about its value. But for some years, I have had the impression the technology is overrated.

Earlier in this decade, there were two incidents:

1. Hype over tech pushed the NASDAQ over 5000. And the bubble burst when the market realized that supporting profits (and value) just weren't there.

2. The second incident was personal; I was deciding if I should get a cell phone. My actuarial side said that the probability of an emergency with no other recourse was too small to justify the cost. I could not put any value on 'buy a gallon of milk on your way home from work'.

Today, I still don't have a cell phone and benefit from the lack of silly interruptions and I always drive with two hands. Don't get me started on bills with 100 line items, multiple-year contracts, roaming charges or warranties on lost, stolen or wet units.

More recently I have turned my impression into a demonstration with simple semantics. Information is not power; knowledge is power. Knowledge is a subset of information that is useful, reliable, statistically credible, pertinent, legally enforceable, usable and applicable.

I'm not talking about the 13th decimal place on a spreadsheet or an Internet search that produces 2.5 million references. As technology makes more information available, knowledge becomes a smaller and smaller subset. We don't have a knowledge super-highway, knowledge technology departments, knowledge science programmers or messages sent FYK. There are only FYI messages.

In the healthcare 'modernization' debate, there's significant discussion about technical advancements, e.g. to define efficient treatment protocols. Earlier generations of managed care providers were successful making changes in this area. But the social and legal environment pushed back on the invasive/intrusive nature of managed care. Whether we have high-tech support for this newest generation of managed care may be irrelevant.

Is Technology Overrated?

I'm certain that techies will disagree with what I've said. Let me try something more palatable. It's not the technology that has value, but how you use it. Would I want an entry level person to text me during a meeting? NOT.

[1] "Why Keep Up With Technology" by Paula Hodges, April 2009 issue of The Stepping Stone.

Originally Published in July 2009 Issue of Stepping Stone

CHAPTER 8
U Cant Rate This, Actuarial Rap – music 1

THE BASS GUITAR starts.

D-do dododo dodo dodo

U cant rate this.
U cant rate this.
U cant rate this.

My my my my system errors so hot
Rate data missing... or not.
Rx rel... not found.
Testing region... is down.
Products and markets... not loaded.
Factor application... not coded.
System session... not bound.
Options... not found.

U Cant Rate This, Actuarial Rap – music 1

U cant rate this.
U cant rate this.
U cant rate this.

Embedded vision ... Medicare D.
Industry tables from A to Z.
Large group, small group, individual rating
Weird activity dates for parallel dating.
Interstate markets... same sex spouse.
Sarbanes-Oxley... not in the house.
Endless variation... without cause,
System enhancements... without pause.
Timing of updates, environment contention.
New procedures but no regression.

U cant rate this.....

There is a sound track loaded under

https://soundcloud.com/tony-batory/actuarial-rap-take-2

If you cant get the soundtrack working, you will have to imagine the bass line which has been used by Ric James, MC Hammer and others.

CHAPETER 9
Y2K = YUK. JOEA – A SCIFI SHORT STORY

THE YEAR WAS 9996 and Joe Amialanczyk was forced to retire. He wanted to continue working the beyond the standard retirement age of 27. Joe liked his actuarial project on Artificial Intelligence (AI) life expectancy and the workweek was cut back to 4 hours so it really wasn't a burden. When he made his request for an extension, his manager first expressed shock which almost seemed contradictory coming from an entity with an Artificial Intelligence. But with the usual instantaneous efficiency, the AI researched, processed, documented and deployed the solution. The request was tersely rejected. Joe had to retire. He never got a clear explanation as to why. Sure, the technological advances of the past eighty centuries had made 'work' unnecessary. It was only a cliched link to the past, some sort of historical remnant to remind everyone just how far humanity had really advanced. Leisure activities were

Y2K = YUK

at the forefront of that advancement and the exploration and exploitation of millions of worlds had provided the fuel for centuries of conspicuous leisure consumption.

Joe felt it was all wrong at a very intuitive level. He did know that his work routine would let him turn those feelings into facts, and create demonstrations from his vague impressions. He also needed his brother Steve's help, not only because of Steve's security access but also for his brotherly emotional support. Joe knew that making Steve understand was not going to be easy.

When Joe returned home, Steve was furiously tapping the keypad on his Zbox 9996.

'What are you doing?' asked Joe.

'Joe-aaaaaa. I'm playing Frock Star Hero against two billion opponents,' replied Steve.

'I thought that every song combination was used up years ago.'

'They've added 64 new instruments, yutk', replied Steve somewhat annoyed.

Joe shook his head. 64 instruments and 2 billion opponents would give him a headache. He grabbed the Zbox unit, pulled it from Steve's palm interface and threw it against a wall. Steve was aghast. He hadn't seen anger in years. Both men almost expected the unit to break but quickly remembered that versions as old as a Ybox 9600 were designed to be virtually unbreakable.

'Joe-aaaaa, what's the matter?' asked Steve.

'Please, stop calling me that.' Joe sighed. 'I'm tired of all these meaningless diversions. When is someone going to stand up and do something worthwhile?'

'What about your date last night? She looked pretty worthwhile,' chided Steve.

'Exactly my point she wasn't real.'

'Huh?' Steve looked confused.

'She told me that she was 126 years old and had 27 children. Well, I tapped Intellinet before they kicked me out of work and she's really 143 years old and has 37 children. She wasn't lying, she just lost track, yutk. Yea she was beautiful but she just wasn't real.'

Steve smirked, 'you and your actuarial life expectancy junk. Gimme a break. If you touch her she's soft, if you squeeze her, she giggles, if you pinch her she yelps. What could be more real? And with that level of experience she must have been pretty good, right?'

'But every date is like that. There's minimum specifications like it was some kind of computer program. It's the exceptions that are special. If there aren't any exceptions then nothing is special.'

Now Steve was really confused. 'Wait a minute. Do you just say they kicked you out of work?'

Suddenly there was a loud explosion outside. It took a full minute before the echoing rumbles subsided. 'What the yutk was that?' screamed Joe. They looked outside but everything looked normal except for dark cloud that appeared to be in the upper atmosphere.

Joe raised his hands tap IntelliNet. But all his inquiries just kept getting referred back to the main menu. "Yutk, see, this is exactly what I'm talking about. Games, dates, vacations, parties but nothing meaningful like 'what was that explosion?'" He pulled his fingers away from the wall monitor in frustration.

'I don't think I ever tapped Intellinet a non gaming question from home,' replied Steve. 'Here, let me enter my security clearance to get into the main database'. Joe knew that Steve's security job was going to come in handy. 'The cloud looks like its in orbit somewhere, the timing would be about right for the regular commercial flight from Gamma Luna. I was working on security for some engineers who were dealing with re-entry problems with the commercial starliners.

They were trying to counter relativistic effects when a ship goes between supra-light speed and sub-light. Even a nano-second at relativistic speed, can cause time dilations. Today was supposed to be the first production flight'.

Joe began lecturing. 'Right, the last thing I was working on was the psychosocial impact of a pilot returning to a world that's years older when he's only aged a few days. That's why centuries ago it was mandated that all pilots have to be AI's, the impact is too much for a real person. Which time period counts towards life expectancy is a function of...'

Steve knew he had to cut him off before Joe kicked into a lecturing high gear. 'I thought it was because the AI's are better pilots,' he joked.

'Will you be serious, suppose someone sabotaged your test flight?'

'Don't be paranoid' replied Steve. 'I used one of the ten thousand Mario security overlays. It would take 4 years for someone to get through that maze. And why would anyone want to? Yutk, more likely that one of your AI's went bananas.'

Joe thought for a second. His studies had begun to show an inverse correlation between AI's advancing intelligence and life expectancy. If one could even call it life. Joe had theorized that psychological imbalances particularly in relativistic dilations, were the root cause. The possibilities were frightening and Joe tried to ignore them. 'Now you're being ridiculous, you know that the basic laws of robotics would preclude any possibility, yutk.'

'You sound like you're trying to convince yourself. Here it is;'

'FLIGHT 546475 GAMMA LUNA/THRAE HAS BEEN TERMINATED', appeared on the wall monitor.

'What does that mean? Ask for more info.'

'Yutk, I can't get through to any real people, there's only AI's on duty. My entire security section went to Super Bowl MMMMMMMMXXIV.'

'But that's not for another 2 yutk months!' wailed Joe.

'Pre-game parties and tailgates start earlier every year. What did you mean when said you were kicked out of work?'

'Mandatory retirement. But my AI psyche profiling project wasn't complete. I asked for an extension but they cut me off'. Joe felt a swelling sense of uneasiness in his gut.'

'Geez, you speak with such pride about your actuarial projects and being an actuary. Why does it bother you when I call you Joe-aaaaa or Joe the actuary?'

'I'm not an actuary any more. I've been terminated,' exclaimed Joe.

'Terminated?' Steve frowned. 'Let me tap something else. Audio monitors, record conversation during the past 15 minutes. System correlate with main security database. Answer the following question. "What's going on?" ' Steve saw Joe's bewildered expression. 'I've had a lot of success with these types of general inquiries in gaming situations. The system will respond with some definitions of the most common words in our conversation and then offer possible solutions.'

'You're NOT supposed to use the security database for gaming.'

'I know, I know. But what would the AIs do if they caught me, fire me? Besides, I can really gain an advantage with the inside info...' Almost on cue, definitions began to appear on the wall monitor.

YUTK – EXPRESION OF DISGUST, FRUSTURATION OR PARANOIA. ROOTED IN COMBINATION OF YUK – EXPRESSION OF DISGUST AND Y2K – ABBREVIATION FOR THE YEAR 2000 COMPUTER PROCESSING ERROR.

'Intellinet Hold!' interrupted Joe. 'I've heard of Y2K. There was widespread fear that computer systems were going to fail because of date errors when moving to a new millennium. But nothing happened, there were no outages, no problems. The whole thing was paranoiac farce.'

'Well' re-interrupted Steve, 'that fits with how yutk describes overzealous fools. Wait a minute, that's it!! The flight engineers were going to counter relativistic dilation using wormholes and gravitation to slow time.' Now Steve began lecturing. 'My Mario security protocols can provide the appearance of advancing time. That's what makes it so effective. It looks like its taking 4 years to get through the maze. If the relativistic counter effect disabled the internal clocks, and Mario advanced local time past the decinnium, the on board Intell could then fail.'

Joe and Steve fell into stunned silence. It was a weird moment given their fondness for lecturing and interrupting each other. Steve could only think of how his security protocols were going to need massive restructuring. He whistled softly thinking of their widespread use. But Joe the actuary saw a much larger, much more ominous picture. The quadrillions of humans scattered throughout the galaxies were overly dependent on technology. Not only the basics needs, like food, healthcare, communications and transportation, but everything even the leisure activities. With humans so focused on their diversions, AIs had all the support roles. Their artificial psyches were subject to a different set of technological problems, a fact that Joe's incomplete studies had just begun to document. A moment of sudden clarity hit him and he realized the awful truth. In a short 4 years, humanity would be facing a cataclysmic disaster, Y10K.

This story was originally published by the Futurism Section of the Society of Actuaries in their 2nd annual sci fi contest. The story won a Reader's Choice Award.

CHAPTER 10
ACTUARIALOGOS

LOGOS AND TAGLINES have been appearing with greater and greater frequency even down to individual units within companies. So, when our actuarial pricing area ran a contest to come up with a logo and even offered a $500 prize, I jumped at the idea. Submissions were supposed to be limited to one but I came up with a dozen so I submitted one power point presentation. (A dozen eggs in the express lane is one item). All 12 of my slides were rejected for various reasons. But as a group, they are quite insightful (or inciteful?) in defining who we are, or at least who I am, as an actuary.

ACTUARIAL PRICING
substituting facts for appearances

1. This was my initial favorite but the intended similarity to military insignia with crisscrossed swords or rifles or sports logos with hockey sticks or baseball bats, was not apparent. The wood pencil may be a passé symbol in today's technical world. I was surprised that many colleagues didn't recognize the tagline. The Society of Actuaries certificate motto has always been a guiding philosophical principle to me.

ACTUARIAL PRICING
only your actuary knows for sure

2. The caduceus reference is common in health related fields. But I wasn't sure how our internal docs and nurses would react to my bastardizing their venerable icon. The pencil as the actual staff may be too subtle. Both this tagline and the previous tagline were intended to raise awareness of the difference between knowledge and information and between fact and opinion. Knowledge is only a subset of information and there is no knowledge superhighway, no Knowledge Technology dept., and no messages sent f.y.k. Too long for a tagline.

ACTUARIAL PRICING
we're on the money

3. Concise and direct but not specific enough. This could apply equally to a number of finance or claim areas.

ACTUARIAL PRICING
difficult is nothing

4. The square peg in a round hole is a classic cliché that really gets the point across. Just ask any pricing actuary to balance competitiveness and profitability. But again it's just not specific enough.

ACTUARIAL PRICING
we do it at the appropriate rate

5. 'Appropriate' has specific actuarial context especially for rate filings, but it is too vague outside of actuarial. The 'time is money' metaphor in the drawing was not apparent.

ACTUARIAL PRICING
the price is right

6. Specific but too many potential problems with stealing the game show name. And I'm not supposed to know the show is on during the day when I work at home. 'The right price at the right time' came out too wordy but raised potential for a future musical logo.

7. This was my second favorite. Our actuarial organization has gained quite an internal reputation for our past success in defining the pricing cycle and staying ahead of it. I also wanted to add a background cityscape to represent Hartford, just to see if our Minnesota and Trumbull colleagues would notice. But the confused personage couldn't possibly be an actuary, else why would she be confused?

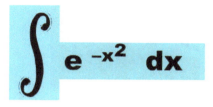

ACTUARIAL PRICING
we do the impossible

8. Too obscure. Many colleagues didn't recognize the integral of the bell curve which has no solution. More pertinent to theoretical math or statistical analysis.

9. Again this relates to our success with identifying trends. But in our company, another actuarial area works more with identifying trends. The Pricing Unit only deploys them.

Shakespeare

ACTUARIAL PRICING

to rate or not to rate, that is the question....

10. This one needs the full Shakespearean butchering including 'Friends, programmers, actuaries, lend me your passwords' and 'It is a tale told by an underwriter, full of sound and fury signifying nothing.' Too long.

ACTUARIAL PRICING
we check the figures

11. This goes back my student days when a shapely colleague 'dropped her prices' right in front of my desk (no cubicles in those days). I responded by spilling a coffee over the entire horizon of my workstation and gained a reputation for customizing financial reports with inkblot-type stains. Since the stains were brown, that said something about the quality of the reports. Today, any figure more graphic than Venus de Milo would be potentially demeaning and harassing, don't go there.

ACTUARIAL PRICING

basically the statistical analysis of the aforementioned trend indicates a proportional tendency toward the contraindicated results of unreliable evidence derived by dubious quality etc, etc., ,,,,,,

12. My favorite, copies have appeared over shared printers and on reference binders.

Sometimes this may be the clearest representation of our role in the organization. An alternate tagline would be 'Actuarial Pricing – nobody knows what the heck we're talking about'.

13. This was the winning entry. Although I would prefer any of my dirty dozen, it is clear and precise. The 'power fuchsia' is directly borrowed from our corporate advertising. But I've never been comfortable with our advertising budget (or anybody else's for that matter). And at the risk of being overly critical, it's a little bland. The decision committee had tough choices and picked a logo that was low risk. Well, corporate, risk adverse, precise, and little bland. That does describe us as actuaries.

CHAPTER 11
The Sunny Actuary – music 2

GIVEN OUR INTERNATIONAL focus, I was struggling long first names. I began to refer to Sakthivial as 'Sak' and to Kumaraguru and 'Kumy'. I never thought this was any kind of slur, geez I don't even like Anthony. But the name that really got me was Sunittaya. She is a programmer from Thailand and uses the nickname 'Nek'. Nek? That comes from a literal translation meaning 'little one' or the youngest in the family. My reaction was 'Sunny' was far better. When we were working on enhancing our rate calculator to do age inside the rating band, I wrote her this love song. No, there was never any serious involvement but the story got passed around. It improved the working relationship between our actuarial area and the programming staff. Humor has productive impacts.

OH, SUNNY,

Yesterday the spec's gave me a pain.
But, Sunny,
You smiled and said the code was easily changed.
Now the testing is done and deployment is here.
The defects we've filed are clear, clear, clear.
Oh, Sunny,
My programmer true, I love you.

Oh, Sunny,
Thank you for the time that you spent with me.
Oh, Sunny,
Thank you for the tests from A to Z.
You gave me more than a helping hand,
Now we can rate **age inside the band**.
Oh, Sunny,
It's so true, that I love you.

There is a sound track loaded under

https://soundcloud.com/tony-batory/sunny

PS If I ever put together a rock or jazz band made up of actuaries, I'd have to call it the RATING BAND.

CHAPTER 12
You Can't Be Serious

THIS STARTED OUT as a 'number of week' trivia contest. We had so many numbers flowing thru our area that we would pick out the most outstanding or unusual item each week. But our area also has a lot of strange, contradictory requests. At staff meetings we would just shake our heads and ask "are they serious?" This evolved into former tennis star John McEnroe screaming at the top of his lungs YOU CAN'T BE SERIOUS. We attached the :-o emoticon. The list would get published semiannually and the staff would vote for their favorite. Here is the list from the 2nd half of 2014.

12/22	Wellness program asks for a download of personal info that is blocked by security restrictions
12/15	Our company stock blows thru $100. What does the price of oil have to do with us?
12/8	Performance review says 'execute flawlessly every time', HR email says 'don't worry about perfection'

Actuarial Jokes, Memoirs and Other Minutiae

12/1   We're in the CT exchange but the bronze plan is $650/month for a $9000 deductible.

11/24   More product issues. Why would people think that's a zip code issue?

11/17   Rating for Accountable Care Organizations needs unique plan codes. Why would anyone think we could use the same plan codes?

11/10   An actuary is a person, who passes as an expert on the basis of a prolific ability to produce an infinite variety of incomprehensive figures calculated with micrometric precision from the vaguest of assumptions based on debatable evidence from inconclusive data derived by persons of questionable reliability for the sole purpose of confusing an already hopelessly befuddled group of persons who never read the statistics anyway!

11/3   A quote's composite age factor is less than any individual factor on the age table.

10/27   Leadership meeting misspelled as leader shit.

10/20   Zip error for a 2010 effective date. Why are we going back that far?

10/13   S-curves for new products nicknamed scurvy or ass-curves.

10/6   Required learning course unintentionally shows the futility of complaining to management

9/29   Invalid Extraterritorial updates. Nobody uses ET.

9/22	Muni code requires a manual override, nobody needs it.
9/15	Uninsured population declining since 2010. What does that have to do with health reform?
9/8	Put in OR changes and now take them out. See 8/11.
9/1	Why do people keep saying that summer is over. It's 92 degrees
8/25	Off the shelf billing application proposed as a replacement for rating.
8/18	IL project finally moves after 6 months. Wait, no it didn't.
8/11	OR network availability is drastically different between small group and large group, like half the state.
8/4	Virgin Islands is exempt from Obamacare Adjusted Community Rating.
7/28	Duplicate row completely disables data upload.
7/21	TX product is statewide. No it isn't. Yes it is. No it isn't.
7/14	What to do with excess cucumbers? Tzatziki. Isn't that Sam's id?
	Plan JRK keeps errorring out
7/7	Billing system charging for children that are on a different policy

Leadshit was the staff favorite.

CHAPTER 13
NATIONAL HEALTH CARE DEBATE 1 – THE REFORMIST VS. THE ACTUARY

CYNICAL ABOUT HEALTH Reform? Who Me?

When a long time friend changed jobs, she lost her insurance. After spending big bucks in the individual market, her spouse got hit with the $43,000 hospital bill after a pre-ex rescission. In the health reform debate, she was on the left...duh. As an activist, she was trying to rally support for various proposals including a Canadian system. When her email distribution hit me, I felt compelled to respond. I was respectful and sympathetic but as an actuary, I wanted to substitute facts for appearances and demonstrations for impressions.

I stated that the risk factors in the U.S. are much higher than Canada so that type of system could not address affordability and that would impact universality in the long run. I pointed out that the proposals do little to address the cost drivers of medical malpractice, lifestyle/obesity and inconsistent treatment protocols. I noted that additional taxes will adversely affect affordability. And administrative expense is too small a portion of the total cost for savings there to have a significant impact. I tried to outline the necessary steps to remove pre-ex and fund sub-standard pools for the very adverse risks. I noted that politicians were unlikely to endorse solutions that would cost votes even if the solutions were correct. In a long chain of emails, my friend continually fired misinformation from undocumented websites and I continually corrected the errors and misstatements. Our email CC list included people from CT to CA and TX to Canada, but they all stayed out of the discussion. Preferring just to watch the two of us slug it out? Or they just didn't care? I tried to reinforce my expertise by referring to my FSA as a PhD since none of the readers knew what a FSA was.

I FAILED. My friend refused to accept what I was telling her. Working for one of those damn insurance companies was too much of an inherent bias. I was 'jaded and cynical'. I 'got mine so I didn't care if anybody else got theirs'. In an effort to demonstrate the difference between cynicism and realism, I offered the following contrast in italic blue type.

As a nation we don't deserve universal coverage. We don't take care of ourselves. We know more about the care and upkeep of our cars than our own bodies. We drive those cars like idiots. We treat each other like dirt both on the street and in the courts. We have no sense of personal responsibility but we do have entitlement mentality and a slew of ridiculously bad habits. A half-assed commitment to reform is not good, because it absolves leaders of the full commitment. Our political and business leaders are only opportunists. Bill Gates and Steve Jobs are not geniuses, they were simply in the right place at the right time. It is a testament to the greatness of this country that we continue to advance in spite of our leadership, not because of it. As the song says 'who would ever, ever want to be king?' It doesn't matter what legislation gets passed because there are lots capable people like myself that are in position to clean up whatever mess comes out of DC. Opinion surveys have limited value because they measure the statistically significant average opinion of uninformed individuals. A federal health system will have the efficiency of the Post Office, the cost effectiveness of the Pentagon and the compassion of the IRS. 'The time for bickering is over' (Obama). Does that mean there was a good time for bickering?

My cynical tirade did help my friend understand that my previous presentations were more factual. But she responded "although you can supply a stream of endless facts, you're missing the point." Note the subtle double meaning of the word stream. What point was I missing, she didn't elaborate. That everyone is entitled to their opinion? Even if it's contrary to the facts? Even if it's irrational? Even if a bunch of Reformists declare our workplace to be a crime scene and mark it off with yellow tape? 30 years of actuarial expertise was unable deal with such intense emotional response to the issues. A doctor's expertise with heart surgery or an engineer's expertise with bridge building had so much more credibility than my actuarial expertise.

I have always admired the way actuaries straddle the separate business, political and academic realities. But not recently. Healthcare reform is a disaster. We're spending millions on administrative political changes that ignore the business and academic realities. I did not bother to continue the discussions with my friend. She would just continue to blow me off. So where does that leave us? Even when we venture from our ivory towers, it's difficult to have an intelligent discussion, let alone a beneficial consensus. And more importantly to me personally than my job or my company's stock price, have I sacrificed a friendship for the sake of my actuarial principles?

Spring 2010

CHAPETER 14
NATIONAL HEALTH CARE DEBATE 2 – THE CONSULTANT VS. THE IN HOUSE ACTUARY

THE DRIVERS OF NATIONAL HEALTH COSTS Originally published in Contingencies Mar/Apr 2009

The national debate over global warming has too much focus on effects and not enough on the causes and solutions. Those poor polar bears on the melting ice floe are getting clichéd. The debate over national healthcare has the same flaw. Yes, there are 47 million uninsured and 16 million under insured. Yes, expenditures impact international economic competitiveness. But these are the symptoms of the problem not the causes. No one can argue against the social equity of covering the entire population. If we were treating a disease, we could use palliative measures to make the patient more comfortable but that will not cure the disease.

Most of the national healthcare debate focuses on transfer payments, who is making them and who has the political clout. But even a historical graph of health expenditures indicates a double digit trend rate that is way in excess of general inflation or GDP growth. National Health expenditures for 2008 reached $2.2T and there are estimates for another $300B for the uninsured.

THE DRIVERS

Let's get to the actual causes of that excessive trend.

Population dynamics - general aging and the baby boomer spike are increasing the intensity and frequency of the major chronic diseases.

Lifestyle – lots of negatives from obesity and diet to the way we drive our cars.

Medical malpractice is out of control. This is the number one item in a doctor's office budget. OB-GYNs are being forced out of practice because they simply can't afford it.

Inappropriate use of medical technology - new devices, tests and drugs can increase efficiency but their application has contradictory objectives like recovering investment cost.

Inappropriate variations in clinical practice - treatments are determined by location not by a proven medical standard. This is also influenced by the mix of specialists and primary care providers in a given area and whether the facility is a teaching institution, public or private etc.

Infrastructure is antiquated and deteriorating. That includes both the brick and mortar facilities and the administrative systems.

Societal mores and standards spur patients to demand treatments that are ineffective. This ranges from antibiotics for viral conditions to experimental procedures for terminal patients. Widespread use of antibiotics reduces future effectiveness.

Coverage mandates add additional cost. State mandated wigs for chemotherapy patients? Federal mandates in $700B bailout bill?

TV commericials for drugs are common. Is this the best way to disseminate unbiased information? There are other sources of other misinformation and outright fraud.

Geophysical risks. Population concentrations increase the spread of infectious diseases.

WORSE IN THE US

Even a cursory look at this list will note the significantly worse US experience with only an indirect correlation to our unique approach to financing. In addition, some drivers invalidate traditional actuarial measures like life expectancy. For example, obesity raises health costs and lowers life expectancy quite independently of the financing system. Is there any country as fat as us?

Per capita expenditures in the US are double other countries even without the uninsured. But 'bang for the buck' can be more accurately measured with the following criteria:

> Patient Safety
> Effectiveness
> Patient-centeredness
> Timeliness
> Efficiency
> Equity

International surveys put the US at the top in Effectiveness as measured by the treatment of specific conditions. We're in the middle for Timeliness but at the bottom for everything else. So what do we do about it?

SINGLE PAYER GOVERNMENT BASED

There is a single payer government based system in the

US. Sure, Medicare is only universal over 65 and new programs like Medicare Advantage go beyond single payer. But we can draw some conclusions after 50 years of operation. Has it been a financial, benefits and administrative disaster? The tax rates are nowhere near self supporting, relying on general revenues and on a hidden surcharge to the private sector called cost shifting. Benefits are incomplete, seniors have to pay for part B and still need supplementary coverage. Benefit design is way too complex; I had a hard time understanding part D myself let alone explaining it to my 90 year old mother-in-law. Various administrative programs have been outsourced to the private sector.

Supporters for single payer say that it does get to universal coverage in the most straightforward way. But the uninsured are only a symptom of the problem. Sure Canada is cheaper but such a system would only have a marginal impact on the above drivers. No, since the drivers are many and diverse, we have to stop looking for a silver bullet.

THE MIDDLEMEN

I did not include the additional layers of current administration in my above drivers. It is true that the employers and the states have a middleman context, but it is questionable whether they contribute to the trend. There would be one time savings in reducing administration that has to be offset by the one time cost of changing the transfer payments.

General Motors has repeatedly said that their health care costs make them uncompetitive. However, it is precisely the costs that their own employees are generating. If we remove GM from the picture and replace their direct expense with a flat corporate tax, their costs may go down. This would be at the expense of other employers, how is that equitable? The bottom line is that neither set of transfers address the drivers.

THE INSURERS

This brings us to the hmos/health plans/insurers. It is a myth that insurer profits have precipitated the crisis. Depending on what time period you use, total profits are roughly $10 billion. That's not in the same order of magnitude as the missing $300B, let alone total $2.2T. The fierce competition between insurers acts a direct check on profit objectives. The impact on trend is not clear.

But as with a single payer system, insurance solutions have to be much more than just downstream check cutters.

THE SOLUTIONS(?)

Each of the drivers has potential solutions of varying degrees of effectiveness and political action. Population dynamics need to be more precisely measured. Every insurance company has risk adjustors for age but they generally do not extend above age 65. With a complete set of risk adjustors, historical population counts and future population projections, even an entry level actuarial student could precisely define the portion of the trend due to aging. More importantly, we need to know when, if ever, does the boomer spike moderate this cost trend? Armed with the population stats, we must create appropriate provider incentives. This would be something much more detailed than "more geriatric specialists and fewer pediatricians."

Disease management ties into population dynamics and lifestyle issues. Preventative care has positive impacts because early detection reduces intensity. Consumer education, lifestyle intervention and disability integration all need considerable development. Utilization review programs have been in place for many years but their focus needs to move away from short term goals like a shortened inpatient length of stay. The entire episode of care, including rehabilitation, followup care, and potential relapses, needs to be considered. All of the above can be combined into a massive effectiveness database that could be accessed both by providers and insurers. But the problem for all the above, is economic inertia.

Substantial capital investment is needed. Allocations in the Economic Stimulus Package for Healthcare modernization are inconsequential. Capital for these programs could come out of insurer profits. But with no immediate impact to the bottom line, they are tough to implement when Wall Street is so focused on next quarter's earnings. The decision for a single payor versus insurance solution may be partly answered by which system can make the most effective use of capital for improvements.

The above should be distinguished from political inertia, for example tort reform is unlikely when Congress is 98% lawyers.

Social inertia also has to be overcome. It is any wonder that the people who tell us that advertising is effective, are the people selling the advertising? Are ads for erectile dysfunction drugs better than telling people that working out and losing weight improves their sex life?

THE ACTUARY'S ROLE

The casual observer may say that I'm biased in favor the insurers because I work for one. Au contraire, I know what they are capable of in the most negative of contexts. I've dressed up the above presentation with some colorful metaphors but in general it's pretty focused on facts not opinions. We do not need more opinions but a clearer understanding of the facts. I would welcome a truing-up of the $300B, $10B and 98% figures, a quantification of malpractice cost as a percent of a provider's operating budget, a way to quantify the present value of intervention programs and detailed population projections that focus on the impact of aging.

Health actuaries have been accused of being insensitive to the issues. In fact, we do so much more than just tacking on 18% to rates each year. There is so much more analysis yet to do.

FOLLOWUP: Several consulting actuaries offered critical remarks so I followed with this response.

This particular article was reviewed by 10 healthcare actuaries and substantial revisions were made to the original draft.

Yes, there are more thorough analyses available but my paper napkin estimate has one major advantage. It's current. It's a 2009 population including a recession generated spike in number of uninsureds and 2009 cost projections taken from the latest National Heath Expenditures report. Here's the numerical calculation (I can fax the original paper napkin complete with coffee stains).

$8200	2009 per capita NHE
x 50M	x 2009 uninsured
x .75	x age/risk adj from the general insured pop
= $300B	= rounded 2009 dollars.

My concern was not with the first 2 numbers but with the 3rd. The uninsured have younger ages but built up neglect. I didn't want get to into a general discussion of risk adjustors in this article; it's a good subject but not on topic. I readily admit this is oversimplified but that's precisely the purpose of a paper napkin. Even a politician can understand the above.

Several studies about administrative expense savings are widely off base. Firm industry estimates have 87% of expenditures going to claim costs. That means that there $300B in total admin costs (derived as 13% x $2.5T), in 2009 dollars. There are significant potential savings but the magnitude of reductions would have to be immense to have any overall impact. At 13%, admin savings can not address the double digit cost escalation. I have represented this graphically by showing a stair step downward on the continuation of steeply trending line. In addition, the savings are one time only, while the commitment to universal coverage is year after year after year.

I hope that fascination with high tech does not demean to value of simpler analysis. I don't recommend this as a standard approach. But in 30 years as a healthcare actuary, I have several high points that were done in elevators, at golf courses and on paper napkins.

Finally, there are two kinds of actuaries. Actuaries that work for insurance companies like myself are sometimes called in-house actuaries. Then there are consulting actuaries, aka out-house actuaries.

July 2009.

CHAPTER 15
NATIONAL HEALTH CARE DEBATE 3 – THE DOCTOR VS. THE ACTUARY

ONE MORNING, I discovered a lump in a strategic area. Having no idea what this was, I jumped onto the company's online consumer education library and searched thru cancers and tumors. It was some time before I found something relevant (true for most internet apps, separate story). First item, I'M NOT IN THE HIGH RISK GROUP. Also, incidence rates are extremely low outside of the high risk group. Great. But then I read this, 'testicular cancer is 100% curable via amputation' and 'amputation is the preferred course of treatment' and 'insurance will pay for a prosthesis.' : (I didn't just go to see my doctor, I ran to see my doctor. He had an opening that morning, I was out the door within the hour and I broke speed limits along the way.

NATIONAL HEALTH CARE DEBATE 3

YOU'RE NOT IN THE HIGH RISK GROUP, is the first thing the doctor says to me. And when he examines me, the lump isn't in the right spot. 'It's likely a distended blood vessel, it's not a tumor. But just to be sure, let's do an ultrasound.' I immediately agreed.

When I got to the xray clinic, I'm the only patient and I have an appointment but I still have to wait half an hour. YOU'RE NOT IN THE HIGH RISK GROUP, is the first thing the techie says to me. But she does the ultrasound and it's negative. A week later the lump is gone! Like it was never there.

First question: how much money did I waste? Over $1000, not including the time away from work.

Second question: how did my attitude change so quickly? I'm a healthcare actuary. I know all about affordability issues, unnecessary tests and 18% trend. Is it simply that when my jewels are involved, you're damn right I want the unnecessary test. Yes, a parochial response is expected, but I was surprised at the suddenness and intensity of the switch. 'NOT IN THE HIGH RISK GROUP' had no impact. And when the tests were negative, my attitude again swung 180 degrees.

Why did the doctor order the unnecessary test? He has 20 years of experience. He has examined 1000s of men. I'm NOT IN THE HIGH RISK GROUP and the lump wasn't in the right spot. He knew it wasn't a tumor. He did not have a financial stake in the xray clinic. So, was the extra test for my benefit, my peace of mind? NO, he was just covering his ass.

What did my employer and insurance company contribute to this episode? Did the tax deductibility of my insurance have an impact? NO. Did the tax efficiency and personal accountability of a health savings account have an impact? NO.

There was a 60% discount on the ultrasound. But with no other patients, volume increases or cost shifting arguments break down. Would transparency i.e. knowing the specific cost of the tests prior to the delivery, have made a difference? NO. Would evidence based treatment protocols or an efficiency rating on my doctor helped? NO.

The consumer education aspect was also negative, it precipitated the entire episode. The goal of consumer education is to help members make rational decisions on how much money to spend, looking at necessity and risk. But the back-end consequences are so horrible that decision making is actually inhibited. Whether the risk is 1 in 100 or 1 in 50 million can not be rationalized in the face of those consequences. Let's be clear, the universe of medical conditions has Alzheimer's, death, and other stuff far more horrible than my limited experience.

This does not debunk consumer education, but perhaps the focus should be on preventive or lifestyle issues. That would leave the decision making to someone who can rationally and objectively evaluate the risk. That's more likely to be the doc and the insurance company, not the patient or family member. In my conversations with the doctor, it was clear that I was knowledgeable. He asked if I had a family history. I told him my only source of information was our online library. His final advice in a stern tone of voice was 'STAY OUT OF THE ONLINE LIBRARY.'

I'm not suggesting that this mere episode be extrapolated to the entire $3T that will be spent in 2014. But there are indications. Recent activity with E coli, flu and other problems have the 'safety any cost' premise. Utilization studies done by Jack Wenberg and the Dartmouth Atlas of Healthcare indicate as much a 1/3 of health spending is unnecessary. If we can acknowledge the social and political aspects of the decision making process, there will be insights on dealing with the financial consequences.

SUMMER 2010

CHATPER 16
NATIONAL HEALTH CARE DEBATE 4 – THE POLITICIAN VS. THE ACTUARY

POLITICIANS ROUTINELY HAVE 'town meetings' to give the appearance that they are listening to their constituency. I went to John Larson's Public Forum on Healthcare Reform. Representative Larson (1st district CT) spoke for only 15 minutes following by 2 hours of questions and answers.

Paraphrased. Rep. Larson is strongly in favor of a public option to fill in the uninsured gaps and increase competition. He is strongly against single payor. He shouted down a bunch of single payor yahoos in the audience. Competition breeds innovation and the country needs the expertise provided by the insurance industry. Insurance is not the enemy but he spoke of insurance cherry picking the risks and how

National Health Care Debate 4

that leads to problems with access. Pre-ex is certain to be eliminated. There are 40,000 insurance people in the 1st district and he seemed genuinely concerned for that constituency. He pointed to record of support for aerospace. When some idiot shouted out 'they're smart people, they'll find other jobs', he gave them a dirty look and moved on to the next question.

There was lots of talk about wellness, prevention, intervention and innovation to bring down costs but no details. There was some inconsistency with preserving the doc/patient relationship.

My question 'what will be done with tort reform?' caught Rep. Larson off guard. After rambling on for several minutes, he finally said 'we must retain the arbitrative system that protects the victim'. My interpretation was no tort reform.

Increase the supply of primary care providers, but no details.

No taxation of employee benefits.

Brand name rx – no support for generics because the manufacturers are all foreign companies. Pfzier is big in CT but not in Larson's district.

The most visceral discussion was on questions over 12 million illegal aliens that clog emergency rooms to get free care. There were audience comments like 'gather up those people and send them back where they came from'. Larson's response who are 'those people? Our parents and grandparents were all immigrants'. The real question is what is our responsibility. Immigration is a big issue but it has to be dealt with separately from healthcare.

Lots of political rhetoric.
The great wheel metaphor – all parts of the wheel must be in place for the wheel to work.

We the people....

In 1787, Thomas Paine said he would not support a constitution with slavery, no women's vote, debtor's prisons and no healthcare. Harpers Review had a good discussion of the problems but it was from 1962.

'The perfect is the enemy of the good'. Political decisions will include compromises but that is better than no decision.

'We need to smooth out the actuarial bumps'. I could swear he looked straight at me when he said that. But what the heck does that really mean?

July 2009.

Followup. There was no followup. No insurance people attended this meeting. Although I emailed this summary to hundreds of actuaries and insurance people, no one responded. I was concerned that the industry insurance was not taking proactive role in healthcare reform. The answer came when we reported record profits for 2014. Healthcare reform was really a non-issue.

CHAPTER 17
BELL CURVE

A FEW YEARS ago, I created over a dozen logos for our Actuarial Pricing area and I was really fond of this one, so I had it transferred to a t-shirt.

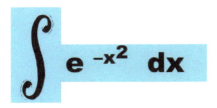

ACTUARIAL PRICING
we do the impossible

But too many of my non-technical friends misinterpreted it and thought it was joke about sex. There is an old math pun about $Se^x = f(u)^n$. But in this case, NO, the squiggly line is not the letter S. The mathematical explanation goes like this.

The integral of a function is the area under the curve. In this case, the function is the bell curve and the area represents the probability that something will happen. Something? Yes the bell curve has many, many statistical and scientific applications. The contradiction is that even though the equation has great utility, it has no solution. That should be distinguished from a problem with a solution that has not yet been found. This thing really is insolvable. Sometime about a 100 years ago, some practical analyst (I would like to think she was an actuary), realized there was no solution and began looking for approximations. Over 100 years the approximations have gotten so good that the problem is effectively solved.

The question for us in 2013 is if we were given this problem today as a new fresh problem, would we ever admit that there was no solution? Or would we spend time and money and resources looking for a solution that does not exist? Healthcare reform has presented us with several no solution type problems. Are we prepared to jump to the approximations?

- Composite rating and the exchanges

- Tobacco and 2 tier rates

- Grandfathered and nonGF rates for a dual option or multioption customer

- Practical display of 46 age rates on quotes and renewal offers

- Rounding

I need a new t-shirt.

CHAPTER 18
IMPRUDENT IMMEASURABLES

THE ACTUARIAL COMMUNITY is sometimes over focused on analysis and data. The purpose of analysis is to aid decision making in an uncertain environment. Forget about specific insurance products or actuarial analysis for a moment and think of general decision making. Our social and business environments are reluctant to take on risk or uncertainty under ANY circumstances. Two clichés keep coming up:

1. It's better to be safe than sorry

2. Stranger things have happened.

Both of these bypass any risk evaluation and are widely used in business decision making.

No one is interested risk evaluation. That's viewed as just someone's opinion, not as an actuarial forecast. A side issue is that an "actuarial opinion" should have more credibility than the average Joe on the street. We have done our profession a grave disservice by using this specific Actuarial Opinion terminology. Consider the wider acceptance if Actuarial Opinion was replaced with Actuarial Forecast.

Take a simple example of system testing. Test plans have become so intricate and over documented that testing actually becomes less complete. When errors result, test plans become even more unfocused.

Take the more important example of medical testing. Certain diagnoses may be literally one in a million scenarios. But we still accept the testing because the end consequences of cancers and other conditions are so horrible. In the case of providers the consequences are malpractice suits. Has this contributed adversely to the health care financials that are under stress? You bet. (pun).

If you flip a coin is the probability of a head = ½? No, not if a head comes up. The probability distribution is deterministic. $P(H) = 0$ or 1. I am alarmed that this 100% deterministic certainty trend is growing. Some of social trend is due to 9/11 and terrorism. Some of the business trend is due to major corporate failures and the resulting Sarbanes-Oxley legislation. So how do I respond when someone hits me with the 2 cliches?

Imprudent Immeasurables

Don't ever cross the street.

Don't ever get into a car or plane.

Don't ever leave your actuarial ivory tower.

CHAPTER 19
ODE TO AN ACTUARIAL STUDENT

I WANT TO query a group of experienced FSA's at an actuarial meeting. Do they miss being a student? I do. Oh sure, I don't miss the intense studying and the pressure. But I miss automatic raises. I miss the study hour which was good for the occasional afternoon nap. Maybe I miss the thrill of the hunt. But most of all, I miss the partying afterwards. Some may say that's just yearning to be younger, which we all wish for. But even my college fraternity days don't compare to some of those post-exam actuarial revelries.

The worse exam I ever took was part 8. I was taking it with two other students who had both failed the exam. Twice. So they were on the verge of being kicked out of the program. As a first-timer, I was thoroughly overwhelmed by the volume of the material. But we studied together and played part 8 Trivia Pursuit, part 8 Jeopardy and part 8 $64,000 Question. Who Wants To Be a Millionaire had not aired yet.

And it worked out well. All three of us nailed the exam. Isn't it strange how for some exams you feel good about the result and wind up with the minimum passing score? For other exams, I've had no clue initially and wound up with a high grade. But this time we knew and the exam was on a Friday so we hit the Hartford night scene.

Hartford is not like Boston or New York. There are some very nice clubs but there is a limit to the number of places you can get thrown out of. One detailed argument was about whether the waiter's tip should be gross or net to the sales tax. Another argument was trying to define a minimum length for a miniskirt in proportion to the total length of the thigh. The theory was taller women can wear shorter skirts, more complex than halfway or "x" inches above the knee. We needed a logarithmic function. Why logarithmic? Because there's an asymptote. But the real problem was data collection.

I woke up the next afternoon on the couch in my friend's apartment, having no idea how I got there. My car was still in Hartford, which was a good thing since I was obviously in no condition to drive. But it got towed…on a Saturday? If nothing else Hartford does have a reputation for towing cars.

When I woke up I had a humongous hangover. On my right fore arm was a tattoo that said 'AMORTIZE OR DIE'. It wasn't a real tattoo: my 'friend' has just drawn it on with a felt tip pen. But it sure scared the heck out of me.

Recently I've gotten some more mileage out of this story when our Actuarial Pricing unit ran a contest to come up with a unit logo and tag line. I considered using 'Amortize or Die' as a tagline. But it conjured up a graphic logo image of a punk actuary or a biker actuary. Those combinations may exist in this diverse universe, but not on our staff. We have a few FSAs with beards, one is even a vegetarian. But the most radical thing our actuaries would ever do is a square root.

All of these reflections now allow me to clearly see the metaphor in Keat's poem "Ode to a Grecian Urn". But instead of the classic Greek figures, I see 2 actuarial students carrying notebooks, calculators and #2 pencils. Frozen in time, they will never see their passing grade, never get their FSA. But the party will go on forever.

CHAPTER 20
TALES FROM INSIDE THE BOX (ELEVATOR)

THE PHRASE 'THINK outside the box' has become quite clichéd and just plain wrong in a number of contexts. Limited capital budgets, system requirements, state and federal regulations all require us to think inside the box. But there's another more literal box. For a colleague's 35th anniversary, I estimated that she spent 3 consecutive weeks on an elevator. Pretty easy calculation. I had to ask, "just what do you do during those 3 weeks?" Stare at the ceiling? Nervously shift your weight from one foot to the other? Idle conversation, the weather is too cold or too hot or too rainy or too dry. My colleague responded "what did YOU do during your 3 weeks?"

One Friday afternoon, I got so engrossed in my work that suddenly it was 5:30. Feeling exhausted, I got on an elevator with 3 other people. The elevator lurched and stopped. None of the buttons had any effect including the one that opens the doors. We called security and they said they are not allowed to do anything except call for an elevator repair person. On a Friday at 5:30? They're probably all at happy hours. They told us to "sit tight", as if we had another choice and as if was enough room to sit. The other people got on their cell phones, called their spouses and began checking emails and stock prices. After about 30 minutes, I had other ideas. I moved to the doors expecting to do a superman routine to force the doors open. The other people screamed "no don't do that", probably expecting we were between floors. With a little tug, the doors opened easily and we were right where we started. Without a word of thanks or any other comment, the 3 people got on another elevator. Not me, no way. I walked down 14 flights of steps. But I did get something positive out of this eventually. I put it on my annual performance appraisal. Major accomplishment for the year, FREED 4 PEOPLE TRAPPED IN AN ELEVATOR. I gave myself high marks for problem solving, seizing the initiative and customer responsiveness. My boss said it was the most entertaining appraisal that he ever read and I got good raise that year.

Elevator service in our old building was so bad, it was one of the major reasons we moved. At a staff meeting I suggested the following to pass the time. When you first get on an elevator, lean over and catch the name on someone's

Tales from Inside the Box (Elevator)

id badge. Then settle back for a bit. When you're about halfway up, suddenly start talking to this person like you've worked with them all your life. You need them to respond to requirements or inquiries and you have tight deadlines, etc., etc. I did this with a woman named "TEMP" and she thought I was crazy.

One of our conference rooms had these ugly pink upholstered chairs. To make things worse, someone spilled coffee on one of seats making a horrible brown stain in a strategic area. For a while, it was fun to go meetings early and watch people's reactions when they would go to use "the chair". Late arrivals were really interesting "Oh, good there's one more chair left…whoops, no there isn't". Repeated requests to maintenance to remove or clean the chair had no effect. I took control, rolled the chair down the hall, put it on an elevator and pressed the down button. We never saw it again. There was no H=hell button, but I sometimes wonder, how far down did that elevator go?

Recently I was driving into work and I had close call with a tracker trailer. Well, maybe not that close, but enough to get my heart beating 220 bpm. When I arrived at the office, my hands were still shaking. I got on an elevator and a woman behind me who I did not know, gave me a rousing "GOOD MORNING!" I almost jumped out of my shoes. I had to cut loose. "What the heck is so good about it, I almost died." The woman was aghast that I could be so rude.

But it really struck me as how cowardly people are. In the privacy of their cars, people will cut you off, make obscene gestures and put your very life at risk. But move them into a person to person situation and suddenly they are courteous and nice. Too bad it never carries over to the highway. Since then if someone holds an elevator door for me, I refuse to get on. "No thanks, I'll take the next one."

CHAPTER 21
A TRIP TO THE GROCERY STORE

IT'S INTERESTING HOW my personal and professional lives overlap. Actuarial/math skills are useful in a variety of personal applications. Try this at the grocery store. As you are putting items on the checkout belt, round them to the nearest dollar and keep the simple dollar total in your head. You can then tell the checkout person your total. When your total is 50cents or less from the actual total, the checkout will swear you have a calculator or a phone app. You can then comment about the statistical INsignificance of pricing everything to the nearest 99cents.

Last week I went to the grocery store for a few things and was amazed at the parallels I saw with being an healthcare actuary. There are no half gallons of ice cream any more. The manufacturers and stores have been reducing the size of the container to hold down price increases. That's not a product improvement, it's simply giving the customer less product. Don't we do the same thing with our high deductible plans? Which would be more obnoxious: the rates for a $100 deductible plan or the price of a full half-gallon of ice cream? The smaller size ice cream container has the same sense of disappointment I get when trying to fill a $3000 deductible.

I was looking for a bag of pretzels. Low salt, no salt, low fat, no fat, no carbs (exactly what are these made of?), gluten free, no gmo, organic, sourdough, hot and spicy, extra crunchy, etc. etc. etc. And the combinations are a factorial function. Who exactly is telling the manufacturers that consumers want more choice? I'm a consumer and I don't want more choice. Or expressed differently, I would like more meaningful choice. Like a bag that costs less than $4. And let's be clear...$3.99 is NOT less than $4. Not statistically, not financially and not actuarially. I began to see parallels with my HSA plan with 14 cents of annual interest earnings, wellness rewards that are based on questionable statistics, and features, features, features that have no meaningful impact. What is the overhead cost of all these choices? More shelf space, more unused/unsold product. The additional administration must be increasing the price.

In the vegetable aisle, the veggies looked great. But by the time I got to the checkout they faded. Is the shelf life less than 10 minutes? No, the veg aisle has special lighting that makes them look better than they actually are. Does that

A TRIP TO THE GROCERY STORE

describe the positive political lighting for Obamacare? But the uninsured population is still significant, cost increases are still trending, healthcare itself is unaffected and the veggies are fading. Which lighting is reality? I walked out of the grocery store without buying anything and left the manager thinking "what's HIS problem?"

Why does my scientific evaluation rebel against marketing baloney? Why does my actuarial science rebel against political science? To paraphrase the FSA motto, the work of actuarial science is to substitute facts for appearances but the work of political science is to substitute appearances for facts. So what should I do about Healthcare Deform, Unform, Nonform, Zipform, Nilform, Nattaform, Underform?

CHAPTER 22
ACTUARIAL INSULTS

THE RECENT TURF war between the SOA and AAA has once again raised questions about need for multiple organizations. The odd result is that the ABCD discipline arm of the AAA has no real disciplinary authority. It will be up to the SOA to discipline their own president for supporting their own point of view. This activity had bad timing as it hit my desk at the same time I was processing my $1200 in annual dues. But on the bright side:

- The dues are tax deductible so roughly 1/3 of the cost is paid by Obama. (thanks to Jim Gutterman for pointing this out).
- If I was a member of 3 organizations, my dues could be $1800 or worse.
- I'm getting 300 emails a year being on a various mailing lists.

All of this does have its humorous points:

ACTUARIAL INSULTS

- How do 2 arguing actuaries toss down the gauntlet? They slap down their pocket protectors. Ok, ok that's too old school. They slap down their cell phone cases. (PS., I don't own a cell phone.)

- How does an actuary get back at another actuary they do not like?

    o He refers him to headhunter as a 'really good prospect'.

    o She quits to work for a state DOI so she can decline everything the other actuary submits.

    o He sends the other actuary an excel virus that divides everything by zero.

    o He white-outs the others AAA certificate to read AA (alcoholics anonymous).

- How do 2 actuaries have a duel? They stand back to back, take 10 paces counting down in odd numbers from 19, turn and fire reserve completion factors or actuarial insults at each other. Here's some insults:

    o You're so nerdy that when your rate filing got approved, you started singing Queen's 'We are the Champions... of the World.'

    o You're such a geek that when your spouse borrows money from you, you charge him/

her interest and compound it daily.

- When you look at appetizers on a menu, you organize it,
  A. shrimp cocktail
  B. stuffed mushrooms
  C. fried calamari
  D. all of the above
  E. none of the above

- When you got your FSA, you replaced the picture of Mr. Spock in your wallet with a picture of Edmund Halley.

- You picked your honeymoon resort because there was an SOA CE meeting that allowed you to deduct the cost.

- You have a mental disorder called depreciation.

- You're so addicted to this that I can call you an actu-holic

- You're so dumb that you think IRS stands for I'm Really Sexy. (alternate question: what do you get when you cross an actuary with a blonde?)

- You refer to the tomatoes in your garden as 'deliverables'.

ACTUARIAL INSULTS

- If your personality was rated, you'd get a premium rebate.

- You can remember 7 computer passwords but not your anniversary.

- You're so mean, your standard deviation is zero.

- Your ego is so massive, it bends light.

- You're so boring, that when people around you yawn, you tell them that they are not getting enough sleep.

I apologize to all you readers that are yawning. You need to get more sleep.

CHAPTER 23
ADVANCED CALCULUS

I KEPT SOME of my old books from college. My favorite has to be ADVANCED CALCULUS by Ellen Buck; that's not just any kind of calculus but the 'advanced' variety. It sits on a book shelf right next to ORDINARY DIFFERENTIAL EQUATIONS and LINEAR ALGEBRA. Advanced Calculus has the proof to the fundamental theorem of calculus on which all integration is based. It has differential transformations and applications to analytic geometry. I signed the book with my nickname at the time, 'Bat', and my fraternity letters, $\Delta\Sigma\Phi$, Delta Sigma Phi. But the book is covered with dust because it has not been opened in many years.

Is the book lonely? Does it feel neglected, deserted, mistreated, abandoned and unloved. Further on down the shelf other books have more prominent positioning but even their use is not recent. LIFE CONTIGENCIES by Jordan, The COMPLETE WORKS OF SIR ARTHUR CONAN DOYLE, a biography of BEETHOVEN and COSMOS by Carl Sagan. No, the books that have been touched recently are The RANDOM HOUSE DICTIONARY, FANNY FARMER COOKBOOK, The AMA FAMILY MEDICAL GUIDE and THE LIVING BIBLE.

But there are many other books that receive lots of attention for a very short time. Although they are bestsellers in someone's marketing definition, they are read once and never referenced again. FIFTY SHADES OF GREY by E. L. James and VARIETY SUDOKOS hold our riveted short term attention but never make it to the book shelf. Such is the fleeting price of fame. Imagine sitting on a plane and the traveler next to you asks 'what are you reading so intently?' ADVANCED CALCULUS? I think not.

The book shelf is far more than a hoarding pack-rat mechanism. It is far more than just a place of honor. It represents my persona, my growth as an individual and as a professional. It is a metaphor for my transformation from a young, idealistic, liberal, graduate student to a conservative, cynical actuary on the verge of retirement. How did this transformation take place? How did I go from STEAL THIS BOOK by Abbie Hoffman and THE DOORS COMPLETE songbook to something so diametrically opposite like a biography of Ronald Reagan. The answers are in those books. By the way, I think someone stole my copy of STEAL THIS BOOK.

ADVANCED CALCULUS is still part of me even though it has no applications to my actuarial work or other hobbies. Far from being lonely or unloved, the book is part of an huge, intense base to a pyramid of knowledge. I think I may take ADVANCED CALCULUS on my next plane trip. If nothing else, it will help me sleep.

CHAPTER 24
ACTUARIAL BUCKET LIST

AS I APPROACH retirement, there is a growing list of things to do before I leave the office that last time. This also applies to people moving to full time telecommuting.

Tie desktop computer to a chair and push down an elevator shaft (pretending to be Bruce Willis in Die Hard). Track progress with laptop.

Toss health reform regulations off roof.

Paint a white board black (Mick Jagger imitation).

Make sculpture or mobile out of 3 1/4 diskettes and cds.

Slam office door several times.

Put up a Whalers poster and play Brass Bonanza (Hartford only).

Burn popcorn in microwave. Find the most unusual/obnoxious flavor of coffee and make 3 full pots.

Spend an entire day playing computer games.

Spend an entire day watching soap operas and game shows, noting that "The Price is Right" fits job description.

Stand at a salad bar and eat lunch on the fly (like John Belushi in Animal House).

Office golf, lacrosse, volleyball and baseball. The real thing, your office or cubicle is the 18th hole, defending net and home plate.

Have loud argument in a conference room with…..**MYSELF**. Make note that the Hartford office address is Asylum Street and I am very happy to get out.